FOR YOU A THOUSAND TIMES AND OVER

AMAN CHHILLAR

Preface

Two souls, separated by miles and worlds apart, find each other through a chance encounter on an anonymous chatting platform. A boy, heartbroken and lost in his past, and a girl, yearning for love and understanding, connect through shared loneliness and pain. Despite the distance, they quickly become a source of comfort for each other, exchanging heartfelt messages, long conversations, and even sharing their deepest dreams. As their bond grows stronger, feelings of love begin to bloom, though both are hesitant to admit it, haunted by past scars and uncertainties about the future.

They navigate the complexities of life, constantly supporting one another despite the struggles that come with their long-distance connection. The boy, burdened by his strict family expectations, and the girl, scarred by past heartbreaks, both carry the weight of their fears, yet their connection remains undeniable. Throughout their journey, they exchange small promises, build trust, and discover the beauty in loving someone without needing to be physically close.

However, as time goes on, their feelings grow deeper, and they both realize that love might not be as simple as they once believed. The story unfolds through moments of joy, heartache, and personal growth, all leading to a transformative realization of what it means to truly love and be loved.

In a world where love often feels fleeting, their story reminds us that true love takes time, patience, and sometimes, a little bit of destiny. Will they overcome the odds, or will fear keep them apart? Their journey is one of hope, growth, and the magic of finding someone who truly understands your heart.

Prologue

Two strangers,
a boy and a girl,
connect on an anonymous chatting platform, each carrying their own emotional scars. Over time, their bond deepens as they support and comfort each other despite the miles between them. Both are hesitant to admit their growing feelings due to past wounds and fears of the future. They navigate their relationship through long-distance struggles, exchanging dreams and promises. As their love blossoms, they learn the value of patience, trust, and vulnerability. Their story is a testament to how love, though complicated, can flourish even when faced with overwhelming challenges.

CHAPTER - 1

" Stranger In The Void "

I'm a shadow in a foreign land,
A stranger in my own two hands.
Friends scattered like the stars at night,
I'm here alone, losing the fight.
The silence screams inside my head,
Anxiety's my closest friend.
I wear a mask, I play pretend,
But I'm breaking where no one can mend.

So I drift into the digital seas,
Anonymous, where no one sees.
Typing words, hoping they'll matter,
In a world that's cold and shattered.

And I cry to the empty screen,
Hoping for someone unseen.
Will they know me, will they care?
Or will I vanish like thin air?
I'm scared to show the girl I am,
Insecure and sinking in quicksand.
But tonight, I'll take the chance to dream,
Even if it's not what it seems.

The world feels so vanilla and gray,
Another stranger just fades away.
My heart's locked tight, I've lost the key,
But still, I long for someone to see me.
Every word I send feels like a prayer,
A whisper tossed into empty air.
Who are you, on the other side?
Are you a ghost, or just another lie?

Still I drift into the endless stream,
Hiding pieces of broken dreams.
In this place, the real feels fake,
But it's the only escape I'll take.

And I cry to the empty screen,
Hoping for someone unseen.
Will they know me, will they care?
Or will I vanish like thin air?
I'm scared to show the girl I am,
Insecure and sinking in quicksand.
But tonight, I'll take the chance to dream,
Even if it's not what it seems.

Then came a voice, soft and strange,
A warmth I thought would never change.
Who are you? Why are you here?
Can I trust, or should I fear?
Your words, they shine, they pull me near,
But the shadows still whisper in my ear.

I'm still that shadow in a foreign land,
A stranger in my own two hands.
But maybe tonight, the dark will shift,
And in this void, I'll find a gift.
Who are you? Will you stay?
Or will this all just fade away?
I'm scared, but I'll let myself believe,
That maybe there's more than I can see.

CHAPTER - 2

" Midnight Confessions "

The clock strikes twelve, the world is still,
I'm lost in words, against my will.
He speaks of love, a tender ache,
A past he'd mend but couldn't make.
His texts, a melody soft and kind,
How can someone this sweet still find the time?
I hide myself behind a name,
A fragile lie, a quiet game.

The screen glows bright, my heart feels bare,
But his warmth feels real, and rare.
I gave him shadows, a borrowed light,
Hoping to keep myself out of sight.

And in the dark, I find a spark,
A stranger who can calm my heart.
No love, no flames, but something true,
A safe place found in someone new.
I gave him a name that wasn't mine,
Still, he stayed, like a gentle sign.
Tonight, I breathe, tonight, I'm free,
To be someone I've longed to be.

We share a world of second chances,
Fragments of our lives and glances.
His sincerity feels so unreal,
How does he know just how I feel?
But the shadows whisper, I hold back tight,
Afraid to show my true face tonight.
Yet his words are a quiet balm,
A lullaby, a fleeting calm.

The hours slip, the walls cave in,
He doesn't know where I've been.
But something in me starts to glow,
And suddenly, I want him to know.

And in the dark, I find a spark,
A stranger who can calm my heart.
No love, no flames, but something true,
A safe place found in someone new.
I gave him a name that wasn't mine,
Still, he stayed, like a gentle sign.
Tonight, I breathe, tonight, I'm free,
To be someone I've longed to be.

Out of nowhere, I let it slip,
My real name tumbles from trembling lips.
He pauses, but his tone doesn't change,
For once, I don't feel so strange.
The night wraps me in soft embrace,
For the first time, I've found my space.

That night I slept, a smile in place,
No racing heart, no frantic pace.
No love just yet, but something warm,
A shelter safe from the storm.
He doesn't know who I am, not yet,
But his kindness, I'll never forget.
Tonight, I breathe, tonight, I'm free,
To be someone who's finally me.

CHAPTER - 03

" Morning Light "

The sunlight streams through my windowpane,
A warmth I haven't felt in days.
It's strange, this calm, this quiet glow,
A little hope I didn't know.
Last night's words still linger here,
A voice that wiped away my fear.
For once, I don't wake up alone,
A stranger's kindness feels like home.

I reach for my phone, a trembling hand,
A message waits, I don't understand.
It's him again, that gentle voice,
A tear falls softly, not by choice.

A Good morning, starting a para with words so kind,
Praising pieces of me I couldn't find.
A stranger's care, so far yet near,
A fleeting joy, a single tear.
No promises, no plans ahead,
Just warmth in the words he said.
For now, I breathe, I let it be,
A new chapter unfolding quietly.

I type my thanks with a heart sincere,
Grateful for the kindness here.
Though miles stretch like endless skies,
In his words, a closeness lies.
I don't dare dream, I don't pretend,
But for this moment, I'll let it mend.
This hollow space, this aching soul,
For now, I feel a little whole.

He's just a stranger, yet somehow not,
A tiny spark in a tangled plot.
I tuck his words inside my chest,
And face the day, I'll do my best.

A Good morning, starting a para with words so kind,
Praising pieces of me I couldn't find.
A stranger's care, so far yet near,
A fleeting joy, a single tear.
No promises, no plans ahead,
Just warmth in the words he said.
For now, I breathe, I let it be,
A new chapter unfolding quietly.

The world still feels like it's out of reach,
But his words taught me what hope can teach.
No grand illusions, no hearts entwined,
But a gentle hand to ease my mind.

The sun feels brighter, the air feels clear,
A small new start, free from fear.
I move ahead, no strings to bind,
But his kindness lingers in my mind.
For now, I live, for now, I try,
With a stranger's light to guide me by.

CHAPTER - 04

" Picture of Seventeen "

Weeks of words, a bond unseen,
A friendship born in spaces between.
But then he asked, so gently, so kind,
"Show me the face behind your mind."
I froze in place, the doubts took hold,
The scars, the fears, the stories untold.
Yet something in me chose to believe,
In the warmth of a stranger I couldn't deceive.

With trembling hands, I took a chance,
A younger me in a frozen glance.
The photo of seventeen, so shy, so small,
I sent it out and braced for it all.

And the silence stretched, my heart grew tight,
Had I done wrong? Was this my fight?
But then his words, so pure, so sweet,
Praised my picture with a kindness so deep.
"You're adorable," he said with care,
And in his words, I felt repair.
No games, no lies, just something true,
A piece of myself he now knew.

I felt a warmth, a glow inside,
A little more safe, a little less to hide.
He wasn't like the rest I'd known,
A stranger, yet I wasn't alone.
I dared to think, "Could this be real?"
But fear still tempered what I feel.
For now, a friend—a place to confide,
Someone to walk with by my side.

The doubts still linger, the past still stings,
But his kindness feels like a gentle wing.
He knows my face, yet not the rest,
But with him, I feel less of a guest.

And the silence stretched, my heart grew tight,
Had I done wrong? Was this my fight?
But then his words, so pure, so sweet,
Praised my picture with a kindness so deep.
"You're adorable," he said with care,
And in his words, I felt repair.
No games, no lies, just something true,
A piece of myself he now knew.

I don't know where this path will go,
But his presence melts the coldest snow.
A friend, perhaps, to share the load,
Someone to meet me on this road.
No promises made, no futures drawn,
Just the present, where I feel less gone.

For now, I'll walk with steady feet,
Each day brighter, each moment sweet.
The girl of seventeen smiles again,
Not for love, but for a friend.
And as the past fades into the mist,
I focus on the now, moments like this.

CHAPTER - 05

" Falling for the Present "

It's been weeks, and now I see,
This feeling's new, it's surprising me.
My heart's a flutter, my mind's a race,
I catch myself smiling, lost in his space.
"Omg," I whisper, pacing the floor,
I've never felt this, I'm wanting more.
Excitement and fear, they dance in my chest,
But right now, I just feel blessed.

He's miles away, yet close somehow,
A warmth that fills my heart right now.
I don't know what the future will bring,
But today, I let my spirit sing.

I think I'm falling, it feels so new,
A nervous joy, a dream come true.
We share our days, our hearts, our skies,
Through pictures and words, no need for disguise.
No promises made, no futures drawn,
Just the present, where fears are gone.
I'm happy, I'm scared, but I'll let it be,
For this moment, it's you and me.

Each day begins with a message bright,
Pictures shared, a streak of light.
Our dreams unfold in whispered tones,
Building a world we'll call our own.
We dream of places we've never been,
Adventures painted on a canvas unseen.
Laughing, loving, hearts intertwine,
Through time and space, you feel like mine.

He tells me his dreams, I share mine too,
A life imagined for me and you.
The miles fade, the distance shrinks,
In these dreams, we don't need to think.

I think I'm falling, it feels so new,
A nervous joy, a dream come true.
We share our days, our hearts, our skies,
Through pictures and words, no need for disguise.
No promises made, no futures drawn,
Just the present, where fears are gone.
I'm happy, I'm scared, but I'll let it be,
For this moment, it's you and me.

In our dreams, he walked at my door,
a knock on the door, where our hearts explore.
what happened next, it's in the next chapter,
it's our movie, we are the main character.
No clocks, no borders, no space in between,
Just you and me, in a world serene.

And as I roam, my heart beats fast,
A feeling I hope will forever last.
I don't know what tomorrow may bring,
But today, I'll let my heart take wing.
We're writing a story, chapter by chapter,
Right now, it's joy, it's hope, it's laughter.
I'm happy, I'm scared, but I'll let it be,
For this moment, it's you and me.

CHAPTER - 06

" A Dream of Us "

He said, "I dreamt of you last night,
A journey that felt so right.
I traveled far, across the seas,
To knock on your door, just you and me."
Her heart raced as he painted the scene,
The door creaked open, it felt like a dream.
There he stood, with a smile so wide,
And without a word, she ran outside.

"I hugged you tight, no space in between,
A moment so real, it felt serene.
You pulled me close, we stood as one,
Our story had only just begun."

He told her, "In my dream, we found a place,
Where time stood still, and love embraced.
From miles apart to a touch so true,
It was just us, the world was you."
As she listened, her heart took flight,
Living the dream in his words that night.
She smiled, she blushed, she felt it too,
Was this dream a glimpse of what's true?

He said, "You called me in, we sat so near,
On your couch, with nothing to fear.
Your beauty glowed in the quiet light,
And I told you how I missed you each night."
Her cheeks burned as she heard his voice,
A story so vivid, it felt like a choice.
The sweat on her brow, her pulse in her chest,
Anticipation sparked, her emotions confessed.

"Our eyes locked, the world fell away,
I leaned in close, no need to say.
Your eyes closed, your lips so near,
And in that moment, we disappeared."

He told her, "In my dream, we found a place,
Where time stood still, and love embraced.
From miles apart to a touch so true,
It was just us, the world was you."
As she listened, her heart took flight,
Living the dream in his words that night.
She smiled, she blushed, she felt it too,
Was this dream a glimpse of what's true?

"In the dream, you sat on my lap,
Wrapped in my arms, no fear, no gap.
Your warmth, your love, your silent grace,
Our hearts beating at the same pace.
We kissed again, as dreams allowed,
The world melted, no room for doubt."
She gasped and said, "Did we just kiss?"
Her playful words, a moment of bliss.

They laughed, they smiled, their hearts entwined,
A dream that reflected what's inside.
Was it just a story, or something more?
A door to love, they couldn't ignore.
As the dream faded, the feelings stayed,
A connection so strong, it wouldn't fade.
The dream ended, but a beginning of something new,
they both understood it, love innit, they both know.

CHAPTER - 07

" Are We in Love? "

Across the miles, his words appear.
Pictures shared, his eyes meet mine,
A moment stolen, a love divine.
He tells me I'm beautiful, his words so sweet,
With every message, my heart skips a beat.
It feels surreal, but I can't let go,
Am I in love? I don't know.

He promises me, "We'll meet one day,
I'll kiss you just like in the dream I replay."
My heart races, my mind takes flight,
Is this love, or just the night?

Are we in love, or is it a dream?
A feeling so strong, yet caught in between.
Every word, every glance, every sigh,
Makes me wonder, makes me fly.
I don't know where this path will lead,
But I want him, it's all I need.
Are we in love, or just the start,
Of a story written heart to heart?

His compliments wrap me in a warm embrace,
He paints my world with his steady grace.
I see the future in his gentle tone,
But I fear the unknown, the seeds we've sown.
"Should I tell him?" my heart softly pleads,
But patience whispers, "Wait and see."
For now, I'll hold these moments tight,
And let the passion guide the night.

We've promised to meet, to make it real,
To share a kiss, to see what we feel.
The passion grows, it's hard to hide,
A tidal wave we cannot divide.

Are we in love, or is it a dream?
A feeling so strong, yet caught in between.
Every word, every glance, every sigh,
Makes me wonder, makes me fly.
I don't know where this path will lead,
But I want him, it's all I need.
Are we in love, or just the start,
Of a story written heart to heart?

The passion burns, it's hard to deny,
With every promise, with every reply.
The way he sees me, the way he cares,
A love like this feels rare.
We've built a world with words and screens,
But it feels more real than any dream.
Our hearts are dancing, slow and true,
But is this love, or something new?

Are we in love? I think I might be,
In the way he makes me feel free.
But for now, I'll let it unfold,
This story, this bond, this heart of gold.
We'll meet one day, our promises keep,
And in his arms, I'll fall deep.
Are we in love, or just the start,
Of a story written heart to heart?

CHAPTER - 08

" Shattered Promises "

Last night, my heart was light,
Dreaming of love under the moonlight.
I was ready to tell him, ready to say,
"You're the one, you've taken my heart away."
I woke up to a day full of bloom,
But his silence turned joy into gloom.
No morning text, no words to see,
The excitement faltered, fear gripped me.

I texted once, I texted twice,
Hours passed, no reply to suffice.
My heart raced, something wasn't right,
The day turned into a shadowed night.

"Sorry, it's over," he finally said,
And the words hit me like a storm in my head.
My world went blank, my soul screamed loud,
Lost in despair, no way out.
I begged, I pleaded, my heart exposed,
But he was gone, his door now closed.
Was it a dream? Was it a lie?
I'm left here wondering why.

I told him, "I love you, don't let me fall,
You're my everything, my all in all."
But his voice was cold, his words were stone,
He left me shattered, all alone.
I couldn't see his face, his tears, his fears,
Distance hid his emotions, his reasons unclear.
All I could feel was the breaking inside,
A love that bloomed now had died.

"Don't leave," I cried, "I need you here,
Without you, my world disappears."
But silence followed, my pleas in vain,
Left with nothing but this aching pain.

"Sorry, it's over," he finally said,
And the words hit me like a storm in my head.
My world went blank, my soul screamed loud,
Lost in despair, no way out.
I begged, I pleaded, my heart exposed,
But he was gone, his door now closed.
Was it a dream? Was it a lie?
I'm left here wondering why.

The promises we made, the dreams we shared,
Now lie broken, I'm unprepared.
Should I end it here, give in to the dark?
Or will the universe reignite my spark?
I stare at the void, tears stream down,
The love I felt now makes me drown.

Was it all real, or just pretend?
A story unfinished, a love to mend?
I don't know where my life will go,
But I hope there's a light in this shadowed glow.
God, if you're listening, guide me through,
Because right now, I don't know what to do.
"Sorry, it's over," echoes in my mind,
But I'm searching for the strength to leave it behind.

CHAPTER - 09

" A New Beginning "

I once had it all, friends by my side,
A girl I loved, my heart open wide.
But one day, she left, no reason, no word,
Just silence and echoes of dreams deferred.
Then the world shut down, locked in my space,
Loneliness became my only embrace.
I carried the guilt, was it something I did?
Her absence became the sorrow I hid.

One night, the weight was too much to bear,
I found myself seeking someone somewhere.
A random chat, no face, no name,
Just strangers passing, all the same.

Then she appeared, her voice so light,
An unknown soul in the quiet night.
I asked her, "What does love mean to you?"
She said, "I don't know, I've never had a clue."
And for the first time, I felt something new,
A stranger's words, but they pulled me through.

She told me her name, but I knew it was fake,
Yet her words felt real, a risk I'd take.
We talked for hours, just two broken hearts,
Sharing pieces, fragile, falling apart.
I asked for her Instagram, unsure she'd agree,
But she gave me her name, a gift just for me.
Though she was unknown, a mystery,
Her presence felt like a kind of destiny.

Why was I drawn to her? I didn't know,
But her words lit a spark, a quiet glow.
She listened, she cared, she stayed on the line,
And for the first time, I felt something fine.

Then she appeared, her voice so light,
An unknown soul in the quiet night.
I asked her, "What does love mean to you?"
She said, "I don't know, I've never had a clue."
And for the first time, I felt something new,
A stranger's words, but they pulled me through.

Her kindness was a mirror to my pain,
Her laughter, a shelter from the rain.
I didn't know if this was real or pretend,
But I felt alive, like I'd found a friend.
For the first time in years, I closed my eyes,
And slept with a smile, no tears, no lies.

Maybe it was chance, or fate's quiet plan,
But she saw through the broken man.
An unknown soul, a name in the night,
Brought back my hope, my will to fight.
And though I didn't know what lay ahead,
Her voice chased the shadows, the thoughts I dread.
A stranger, a spark, a story unplanned,
In her words, I found where I could stand.

CHAPTER - 10

" A Spark of Hope "

The morning sun rose, but it felt brand new,
For the first time in years, I knew what to do.
I typed out my heart, let the words unfold,
A message of warmth, a kindness untold.
I hadn't seen her, she was just a name,
But her voice lit a fire, a soft steady flame.
I praised her beauty, though I couldn't see,
Because her words had already meant so much to me.

I sent the message, nervous, unsure,
Would she reply or leave me insecure?
But deep in my heart, I held on tight,
Hoping my words would brighten her night.

Then her reply came, sweet and sincere,
A message so kind, it brought me to tears.
For the first time, someone cared to see,
The broken boy that still lived in me.
Her words were a melody, soft and true,
And in that moment, I felt something new.

She answered my kindness with beauty and grace,
A stranger's affection lit up my space.
Through screens and miles, her soul shined bright,
She returned my warmth in the quiet night.
I didn't know if this was fate or chance,
But her words gave my tired heart a new dance.
I still carried my pain, my scars ran deep,
But her kindness woke something I thought was asleep.

I wanted to be the reason she'd smile,
To make her feel cherished, even for a while.
Through every text, I poured my care,
Hoping she'd feel how much I was there.

Then her reply came, sweet and sincere,
A message so kind, it brought me to tears.
For the first time, someone cared to see,
The broken boy that still lived in me.
Her words were a melody, soft and true,
And in that moment, I felt something new.

A stranger who saw what others ignored,
Who answered my kindness and gave me more.
She didn't judge, she didn't ask,
She just listened and gave me a task.
"Make her smile," my heart quietly said,
And so I focused on her instead.

Though my past pain lingered, her light broke through,
A flicker of hope, something fresh and true.
She was just a name, a voice, a screen,
But she became the kindest soul I'd ever seen.
I didn't know where this would lead,
But in her friendship, I found what I need.
A spark of hope, a bond untold,
A stranger's care, worth more than gold.

CHAPTER - 11

" A Dream of Love "

Weeks have passed, her name feels like home,
A place I return to, where I'm not alone.
I feel something stirring, but I'm so afraid,
The scars of my past haven't yet fully faded.
Last night I dreamed of her, it felt so real,
Her laughter, her touch, the warmth I could feel.
I kissed her softly, held her close in my arms,
Her presence in my dream felt like a charm.

Morning light broke, and I sat there still,
Was this my heart or my mind's quiet will?
I was scared to admit what I'd come to know,
But a part of me didn't want to let it go.

Should I tell her about the dream I had?
Would she laugh, or would she be glad?
I feared her response, but her heart felt safe,
So I shared my dream, and her love embraced.
Her sweet reply melted my fear,
For the first time, the future felt clear.

Her words came back with a softness, a glow,
A warmth in her voice, like the first fall of snow.
She listened, she cared, she didn't make light,
Her gentle response made everything feel right.
I knew she could sense what I couldn't say,
That my walls were crumbling in her own quiet way.
Trusting her brought me peace and rest,
In her kindness, I found my heart's best.

But questions lingered, "Should I take the leap?
What if I fail? What if it's too steep?"
Yet her love felt steady, like a calm, gentle tide,
And my fears began to slowly subside.

Should I tell her about the dream I had?
Would she laugh, or would she be glad?
I feared her response, but her heart felt safe,
So I shared my dream, and her love embraced.
Her sweet reply melted my fear,
For the first time, the future felt clear.

In her voice, I found the courage I lost,
In her trust, I learned to pay the cost.
She's not just a dream, not just a thought,
She's a light in the dark I never forgot.
Maybe it's love, maybe it's more,
Maybe she's the key to unlock my door.

Now I'm standing on the edge of the unknown,
With a heart that feels lighter, less alone.
Should I approach her, take the chance?
Or let this be just a fleeting romance?
For now, I'll hold her close in my dreams,
And cherish the peace her presence brings.
One day, maybe, I'll find the words to say,
That she's the light that's guiding my way.

CHAPTER - 12

" Caught In Two Minds "

Weeks turned to months, and I found my way,
In her smile, her voice, the words she'd say.
She sent me her world, piece by piece,
A photo, a laugh, a moment of peace.
I was ready, my heart knew what to do,
To tell her my love was pure and true.
But the night fell heavy, a shadow loomed,
Unseen, a storm was coming soon.

I dreamed of her face, the joy she'd bring,
Unaware my world was unraveling.
My heart was steady, my soul was clear,
But fate had other plans, so severe.

"Choose," my father said, his voice like stone,
Between blood and love, I was left alone.
Tears fell like rivers, my chest caved in,
How could I break her, how could I begin?
Caught in two minds, I hardened my heart,
But losing her tore my world apart.

The confrontation burned, words like knives,
My secret love laid bare, changing our lives.
His words were final, no room for debate,
Trapped between duty and a cruel twist of fate.
I messaged her trembling, my heart on the floor,
Begging her to leave, to love me no more.
Her innocence pure, her love so kind,
I cursed the world that forced me to blind.

I cried for hours, my soul felt torn,
For the love I found, for the ties I'd worn.
I knew what she meant, she'd become my light,
But now I was drowning in endless night.

"Choose," my father said, his voice like stone,
Between blood and love, I was left alone.
Tears fell like rivers, my chest caved in,
How could I break her, how could I begin?
Caught in two minds, I hardened my heart,
But losing her tore my world apart.

Her face haunted me as I typed those words,
Each letter a dagger, each syllable burned.
"Never see me again," I wrote in despair,
But my love for her still hung in the air.
I knew in that moment what she meant to me,
But love and duty weren't meant to agree.
I chose the path they carved in stone,
And left my heart to grieve alone.

That moment, I shattered, I lost my way,
The brightest love now slipping away.
She was my peace, my solace, my dream,
But the weight of the world tore us at the seams.
Now I sit in silence, her name a prayer,
Wondering if she feels my love in the air.
For what else could I do, bound by my fate?
I broke her heart, and sealed my own in hate.

CHAPTER - 13

" A Love That Lingers "

The nights were long, the days were gray,
Her face in my mind, it wouldn't fade away.
"What have I done?" was all I could say,
Her voice, her laugh, seemed so far away.
My father's words still echoed near,
"Focus on your future, love has no place here."
But my heart rebelled, it wouldn't align,
For in my soul, she was still mine.

Weeks turned to months, the silence grew,
But her shadow lingered, I always knew.
I couldn't move on, couldn't let her go,
Her pain, her smile, still made my heart glow.

So I reached for her, trembling, afraid,
Would she forgive the mess I made?
Just one message, a desperate plea,
"Are you okay? Can you talk to me?"
The reply came swift, her words like a balm,
In her voice, I found my calm.
As friends, we stood, rebuilding what fell,
A bond that no distance could quell.

Her kindness remained, though I'd broken her heart,
She welcomed me back, a fresh new start.
Though oceans lay between her and me,
I vowed to protect her, whatever may be.
I sacrificed sleep, time, and emotion,
To show her she mattered, to prove my devotion.
It wasn't love I could openly show,
But a quiet resolve to never let her feel low.

She smiled again, and my world turned bright,
Her laughter brought warmth to the coldest night.
Though my heart still yearned for what we could be,
I chose her happiness over my plea.

So I reached for her, trembling, afraid,
Would she forgive the mess I made?
Just one message, a desperate plea,
"Are you okay? Can you talk to me?"
The reply came swift, her words like a balm,
In her voice, I found my calm.
As friends, we stood, rebuilding what fell,
A bond that no distance could quell.

I made a vow, though unspoken and quiet,
To care for her through storm or riot.
Her joy became my secret goal,
Her peace of mind, my heart's sole role.
No matter the cost, I'd bear the weight,
To keep her safe, to guard her fate.

Though love seemed distant, a dream untold,
I cherished her presence, more precious than gold.
The boy who was broken found his way,
In caring for her, he found his stay.
And though the future remained unclear,
For now, he'd stand, always near.
With every word, he'd silently pray,
That her happiness would never stray.

CHAPTER - 14

" Hope in the Shadows "

When he vanished, my world turned gray,
The colors of life faded away.
I stared at the ceiling, nights felt so long,
Broken and fragile, trying to stay strong.
Thoughts crept in, dark as the night,
But a whisper of hope kept me in the fight.
I held on to the memory of his eyes,
The love they held, the truth in his lies.

And just when I thought I'd lost my way,
A message popped up like the dawn of day.
I froze in my steps, my heart skipped a beat,
His name on my screen felt so bittersweet.

When he vanished, my world turned gray,
The colors of life faded away.
I stared at the ceiling, nights felt so long,
Broken and fragile, trying to stay strong.
Thoughts crept in, dark as the night,
But a whisper of hope kept me in the fight.
I held on to the memory of his eyes,
The love they held, the truth in his lies.

And just when I thought I'd lost my way,
A message popped up like the dawn of day.
I froze in my steps, my heart skipped a beat,
His name on my screen felt so bittersweet.

He came back, like a dream I'd replayed,
Tears fell as I read the words he'd conveyed.
Was he here for me, to mend what broke?
I clung to his words, to the love they evoked.
If he can't be mine, then I'll stand by his side,
For even as friends, he's my heart's guide.

His voice felt like sunlight after the rain,
He explained his silence, his heartbreak, his pain.
"My father's words were chains I couldn't defy,
But I couldn't let go, so here am I."
I listened, each word a balm to my soul,
Understanding his struggle, his heart's control.
If being just friends was all we could be,
I'd accept it with grace, though it tortured me.

For in his voice, I found my peace,
A love unspoken that would never cease.
Even if the world wouldn't let us align,
I'd treasure this bond, both his and mine.

He came back, like a dream I'd replayed,
Tears fell as I read the words he'd conveyed.
Was he here for me, to mend what broke?
I clung to his words, to the love they evoked.
If he can't be mine, then I'll stand by his side,
For even as friends, he's my heart's guide.

I'll take what I'm given, his laughter, his care,
Even if love can't flourish, I'll still be there.
A connection so pure, it defies every rule,
Though my heart aches, I'll keep it cool.
I'll hold his secrets, I'll share his pain,
And quietly hope we'll meet again.

He's here, though not how I dreamed he'd be,
But his presence alone sets my spirit free.
I'll love him in silence, a love undefined,
For even in pieces, our hearts are entwined.
As friends, we'll carry this fragile thread,
A bond unbroken, though words are unsaid.

CHAPTER - 15

" Behind the Curtain "

Weeks have passed, and they're back once more,
Not as lovers, but as friends to the core.
Bound by the miles, by time zones apart,
Yet bound by a love they can't voice in their hearts.
He calls her at night, she listens in peace,
In the quiet of friendship, their longing won't cease.
The wounds of the past, though deep, start to fade,
As they care for each other in this masquerade.

Behind the curtain, love quietly stays,
Hidden in whispers, in unspoken ways.
They're both too scared to reveal the flame,
Afraid that the past might happen again.
But look at the gift, the cruel, tender art—
Two hearts in love, yet playing their part.

He loves her deeply, but silence is his shield,
A fear of the distance that life has revealed.
So he gives her his care, his warmth, his time,
Calling her his friend, though it feels like a crime.
She loves him too, but holds back her tears,
Afraid of rejection, reliving her fears.
So she comforts him, mends his frayed soul,
Playing her part, though love takes its toll.

Behind the curtain, love quietly stays,
Hidden in whispers, in unspoken ways.
They're both too scared to reveal the flame,
Afraid that the past might happen again.
But look at the gift, the cruel, tender art—
Two hearts in love, yet playing their part.

Oh, the irony of love's fragile thread,
Two souls connected, too afraid to be said.
Their every laugh, their every sigh,
Speaks the truth they both deny.
In the silence, their hearts intertwine,
Each longing to cross the invisible line.

Will they step out, let the curtain fall?
Or will fear keep them from it all?
For love is a gift, though it comes with its pain,
A bittersweet joy, a tender chain.
Two hearts in hiding, yet closer than near,
Playing their parts in a love they revere.

CHAPTER - 16

" The Moment I Dreamed Of "

It's been months, and I'm happy again,
Yet questions linger, driving me insane.
Does he love me, or am I reading too deep?
His efforts, his care—into my heart they seep.
No one else would do all that he's done,
But uncertainty looms like a shadowed sun.
I tell myself, "Just live for today,
Don't worry if love fades or stays."

And then that day, just like the rest,
We talked, and my heart confessed.
The tone grew soft, emotions grew near,
And what he said next—I'll always hear.

"I love you, yes, I do,
I'll stand by you, I'll see us through.
Will you be my life partner, my forever, my own?"
His words hit my heart like the sweetest tone.
The world stood still, I couldn't breathe,
A moment so surreal, I couldn't believe.

I froze in place, my mind went blank,
Tears welled up, and my heart sank.
The day I dreamed, the words I craved,
Were spoken so purely, my soul was saved.
Pinching myself, "Is this even real?"
Ten times over, just to feel.
Then I jumped, crying in delight,
It was the most beautiful moment of my life.

"I love you too, yes, I do,
You're my dream, my heart, my truth.
Forever and always, I'll stand by you,"
I said through tears, my joy breaking through.
The stars aligned, the night was ours,
A love story written in cosmic hours.

All the pain, the wait, the fear,
Faded away as his love drew near.
The boy I doubted, the one I admired,
Now spoke the words my heart desired.
Two souls divided by distance and fate,
Now united in love, it wasn't too late.

That night ended, but it's just the start,
Of a journey together, hand in heart.
From friends to lovers, we've come so far,
He's my forever, my brightest star.
And now I know what love can do,
Because it brought me him, and it feels so true.

CHAPTER - 17

" A Brave Heart's Confession "

I'm happy now, I feel alive,
But there's a void I can't describe.
She's my dawn, my midnight light,
Yet something feels just out of sight.
We talk for hours, like we always do,
But tonight, emotions pierce right through.
She's given me so much, her sleepless nights,
Her care, her love—she's my guiding light.

For the first time, my future is clear,
Her smile's the vision I hold dear.
But fear grips me, what if I fall?
What if she doesn't feel it at all?

"It's now or never," my heart says strong,
I've waited for this moment for so long.
"I love you," I write, my soul exposed,
With trembling hands, my heart enclosed.
The minutes stretch, silence fills the air,
What if she leaves? What if she's not there?

Five long minutes, my world on pause,
Every second feels like a loss.
Then her reply, her words so sweet,
Brought my heart back to its steady beat.
"I love you too," she says with grace,
"Yes, I'll be your partner, your safe place."
Tears of joy stream down my face,
Thanking the stars for this love's embrace.

I promise her now, I promise her then,
To love her forever, again and again.
Through all the storms, through every trial,
I'll stand by her with every mile.
Tonight's the night my dreams came true,
She's my forever, my skies so blue.

With a heart at peace, I lay my head,
The happiest boy the world has bred.
Her love's my anchor, my guiding star,
I'll hold her close, no matter how far.
And as I sleep, I thank above,
For giving me her, my one true love.

CHAPTER - 18

" When Love Wins Over God "

The sun rose high on a fateful day,
Two hearts met, miles away.
Shy smiles exchanged, yet joy so clear,
No distance or time could interfere.
What began as a random, fleeting chance,
Became a love, a timeless dance.
In a world where love fades like fleeting flame,
Their story stood strong, a cherished name.

When love wins over fate and fear,
It bridges gaps, brings hearts near.
In a world that changes, breaks, and bends,
True love is where the story mends.
Destiny played its gentle part,
To bring together two loving hearts.

No time zones now, no walls in between,
Their love's a castle where dreams convene.
They saw the battles, they bore the scars,
Yet here they are, under the same stars.
For love that's pure can make the world bow,
It turns every "why" into a sacred "how."
Parents' blessings came with time,
As love's melody sang a rhyme.

In a fleeting world, they proved it's real,
A love so deep you can only feel.
From strangers to soulmates, across the tide,
Their love was the ship, and God was their guide.

When love wins over fate and fear,
It bridges gaps, brings hearts near.
In a world that changes, breaks, and bends,
True love is where the story mends.
Destiny played its gentle part,
To bring together two loving hearts.

In a sea of hearts that drift and sway,
Theirs anchored strong, never led astray.
Through storms of life, through moments grim,
Their love was the light that never dimmed.
A random chat, a spark divine,
Led to a future, a perfect design.

Now they stand, hand in hand,
A love that destiny had planned.
Through the doubts, the pain, the tears,
They conquered all, embraced their fears.
Their love whispers a tale so true,
Hold on tight, and it'll guide you through.

Not all stories have a happy end,
But when love is pure, even hearts mend.
They taught us this: through trials and strife,
True love's the compass, the light in life.
From random chats to vows they swore,
When love wins over God, it soars.

CHAPTER - 19

" The Final Step "

I look at myself in the mirror, eyes so tired,
A heart full of nervousness, emotions uninspired.
Why does it always happen to me?
I ask, my voice breaking, a quiet plea.
The dress, not ready, the nerves take their toll,
As the phone rings, it echoes through my soul.

It's the day I've waited for, yet here I stand,
Nervous, unsure, with trembling hands.
But the voice on the phone, it calls me near,
And I hear him softly, wiping my tears.
"Don't worry, love, it's our day to shine,
You'll walk down that aisle, everything will be fine."

The dress is ready, my heart starts to race,
Excitement and joy fill the empty space.
It's the moment we've dreamed of, after all this time,
Two souls united, a love so divine.
With a garland in hand, I stand before him,
Eyes glistening with tears, love's song to begin.

It's the day I've waited for, yet here I stand,
Nervous, unsure, with trembling hands.
But the voice on the phone, it calls me near,
And I hear him softly, wiping my tears.
"Don't worry, love, it's our day to shine,
You'll walk down that aisle, everything will be fine."

He puts the vermilion on my head,
And I feel the promise, all that's been said.
In that moment, we know it's true,
No more waiting, just me and you.
Through all the struggles, we've come so far,
From strangers to soulmates, now we are who we are.

We stand together, tears in our eyes,
A love so deep, it will never die.
The garland exchanged, our vows we share,
A bond unbreakable, beyond compare.
I smile at him, and he smiles too,
We made it through, our love stayed true.

It's the day I've waited for, and here I stand,
With the love of my life, hand in hand.
No more doubts, no more fears,
Just forever together, through the years.
"Don't worry, love, it's our day to shine,
You've been mine, and I'll always be thine."

So here we are, standing side by side,
No more distance, no more divide.
True love has conquered, we've come this far,
Our hearts forever, just as they are.
We did it, my love, we made it through,
And now it's just me and you.

" For You A Thousand Times And Over "
said Aman,

" Bareh Tu Hazar Dafaa."
replied Parinita ...